HOME TO ME

Poems Across America

Selected by LEE BENNETT HOPKINS
Illustrated by STEPHEN ALCORN

Orchard Books ◆ New York
An Imprint of Scholastic Inc.

Thanks are due to the following for use of works especially commissioned for this collection: Curtis Brown, Ltd., for "A Place Called Prairie" by Rebecca Kai Dotlich, copyright © 2002 by Rebecca Kai Dotlich; "City I Love" by Lee Bennett Hopkins, copyright © 2002 by Lee Bennett Hopkins; "By Edge of Sight" by Jane Yolen, copyright © 2002 by Jane Yolen. All reprinted by permission of Curtis Brown, Ltd.

Marian Reiner for "On My Island" by Patricia Hubbell, copyright © 2002 by Patricia Hubbell. Used by permission of Marian Reiner for the author.

All other commissioned works are used by permission of respective poets, who control all rights: Joseph Bruchac for "Rez Road"; Sandra Gilbert Brüg for "Needed"; Sharon Darrow for "First Saturday Morning"; Lillian M. Fisher for "My Desert Home"; Joan Bransfield Graham for "Wildwood by-the-Sea"; Fran Haraway for "Mountain Ramble"; Tony Johnston for "Milking"; C. Drew Lamm for "Rocking House"; Ann Whitford Paul for "Walking Home from School"; Alice Schertle for "Christmas Tree Farm"; Janet S. Wong for "Living Above Good Fortune."

LIBRARY OF CONGRESS CATALOGING-IN-PUBLICATION DATA
Home to me : poems across america / selected by Lee Bennett Hopkins ; illustrated by Stephen Alcorn.   p. cm.   Summary: A collection of fifteen poems by various authors about home, whether it is on a boat, in a trailer park, on a reservation, or in a small town.
ISBN 0-439-34096-9
1. Home—Juvenile poetry. 2. Children's poetry, American. [1. Home—Poetry. 2. American poetry—Collections.] I. Hopkins, Lee Bennett. II. Alcorn, Stephen, ill.
PS595.H645 H66   2002   811.008'0355—dc21   2001036975

10 9 8 7 6 5 4 3 2 1   02 03 04 05 06

Printed in Mexico 49 • First edition, September 2002 • Book design by David Caplan

For Rebecca M. Davis—
who always makes me feel at home.
— L. B. H.

Al Maestro Marco Lukolic, continua e
nobile fonte d'ispirazione. Con profonda
ammirazione e gratitudine.
— S. A.

CONTENTS

EDITOR'S NOTE

Where we live — the place we call home — strongly influences our way of life.

Whether one lives on a prairie where a child ". . . pedals through grasses/bone dry, needle thin", a reservation where "Mother Earth is always beneath our feet", or a city where one wakes up to hear "sputters/of sweepers/swooshing litter/from gutters", home is an integral part of growing up, being, becoming.

Home to Me features fifteen commissioned works by contemporary poets who reside in geographical areas as diverse as a Christmas tree farm in New England and a desert home in the Southwest.

Stephen Alcorn's majestic paintings capture each of these environments, showing the wide, rich landscape of life in America.

Home to Me reveals home and heart, the pulse that makes our country so unique — the beat that makes us all individuals — yet one.

LEE BENNETT HOPKINS
Scarborough, New York

A Place Called Prairie

I pedal
   through grasses
      bone dry, needle-thin,
         passing warriors of bitter winds;
       blazing star
        and prairie rose.

       Biking on paths
        of powdered rock
         I stop, drag my toes
        through slow,
            s l o w
                 waters
        that ribbon, run,
        ramble along;

        from a distance
        I watch warm winds
        play spring games
           in open yards,
        tossing strings
        of snow-white sheets
        to tumble, flutter, flap
        in plum-colored skies—

       I breathe in stories
        told to me;
       when winds came calling,
      a fine dust falling
     on these same
      prairie plains.

    ❋ *Rebecca Kai Dotlich*

WILDWOOD BY-THE-SEA

What do I like best
about the sea?
        The sound of it—
crashing, smashing
        pound of it,
push and pull
        call of gulls,
hypnotic hush,
        quiet lull.

What do I like best
about the sea?
        The sight of it—
leaping, curling
        might of it,
back and forth each
        lacy boom,
how it lures
        sun and moon.

What do I like best
about the sea?
        The smell of it—
fishy docks,
        salty spray—
where people play
        in the ocean,
air is slick with
        coconut lotion.

What do I like best
about the sea?
        The feel of it–
how it cools me
        in the heat,
how it sweeps me
        off my feet,
buoys me—
        my mind floats
free.

What do I like best
about the sea?
        The taste of it—
boardwalk's bounty—
        pizza, fries—
taste better under
        salty skies.

What do I like best
about the sea?
        The fact that
it belongs
        to ME!

✳ *Joan Bransfield Graham*

- 14 -

ON MY ISLAND

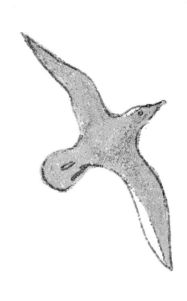

I watch sleek seals on wave-wet rocks,
rowboats bobbing at weathered docks.

I hear the buoy's lonely bell,
I touch a chalky oyster shell.

All about me, pines grow tall.
All about me, seagulls call.

I dream of sunken ships, dim caves,
mermaids floating on sunlit waves,

then wake to silver everywhere—
fog drifting through my island air.

I long, sometimes, to go away,
and other times, just want to stay

on my island far at sea,
this island—home to me.

✳ *Patricia Hubbell*

By Edge of Sight

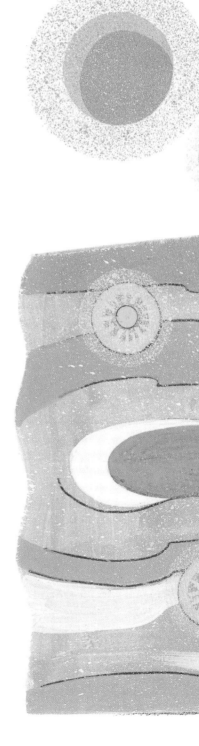

At the water line,
At the start of night,
I see what's mine
By edge of sight.

A single loon
Writes a word in its wake.
A crescent moon
Wrinkles lake.

A shadow lifts
From lake and flies,
Like a rising mist
Before my eyes.

Firefly lights
Signal off, then on.
I blink a response,
Then day is gone.

All my life I'll see
My world this way,
By edge of sight
At the end of day.

 Jane Yolen

ROCKING HOUSE

When I was young my mother rocked me
her rocking chair waves on maternal sea.
I slept to a rhythm deep inside
ebb and flow—briny night ride.

When I was older we moved to this boat
that rocks all night—holds me afloat.
In morning light I stretch, rise
still held tight while riding tides.

Sun from sea washes my walls.
Sky-spawned rain spills waterfalls.
Ocean below me, I drift above fish.
Cast a pebble from my window. Make a wish.

Water stars shimmer up from the deep
Moon above, beneath while I sleep.
A rocking boat bed that holds my dreams,
my tears, my fears, my in-betweens.

I'm now too heavy for a lap to hold
no one rocks a child this old.
Yet every night I sway in sea air
rocked aloft by Neptune's lair.

Held in my bed in the bow of my boat
in the hold of my ship, home I float.
Buoyed, tossed, swayed by ocean's flow
a gift to grow up this wild and slow.

Like reins on a horse as it canters the moors
or string on a kite while it soars
I tie my house to the end of the pier
so when I come home, it will still be here.

As I set my own sails, make my way
anchor pulled up, inner compass in play
thrum of billow, seasoning of sea
my rocking house harbor now rides inside me.

※ *C. Drew Lamm*

FIRST SATURDAY MORNING
BEAUMONT, TEXAS

On oyster shell and palm tree lanes,
our new neighbors' trailers, humpbacked

mildew-streaked beached wanderers,
surround ours, muddy with road-splash.

Sunlight bright on ocean air, mid-morning,
country music blares through screen doors.

Mama, in pink curlers, hums along,
sets terra-cotta pots of peppermint

carnations on our trailer hitch.
Daddy with long-handled scrub brush

hoses down the roof. From above,
his footsteps' hollow thrum,

swish, splash of brush and water.
My sister rides bikes with her new friend,

singing her way toward seesaw and swings.
In the space between friends,

I sit in black walnut tree shade,
bark scratching through my shirt,

drone of heavy-winged bee, black-striped
yellow fur against blue hydrangea,

damp earth cool brown, smooth
under saw-toothed leaves, remember

last Saturday's desert-dust front yard,
my best friend's laughter out her kitchen window,

West Texas sunset-streaked sky, turquoise,
one silver star rising from evening's deep horizon.

❋ *Sharon Darrow*

MY DESERT HOME

Here on Table Mesa
I look down on endless sand
That seems to spread forever
Over barren lonely land.
My home is on the stony ridge
Of a prehistoric sea
Where brittle bushes shine their gold
In shade of a single tree.
A cactus like a one-armed man
Is pointing to the sky.
Above the distant canyons
Hawks and eagles fly.
My wilderness is far away
From noisy speeding cars.
The only lights I see at night
Are from a moon and stars.
Secret silence fills all space
On this lonely desert shelf.
Where solitude restores my soul
I come to know myself.
Whatever changes life may bring
What ill may come along,
This land is where I'll always stay
It's here that I belong.
My home is on the stony ridge
Of a prehistoric sea
Where brittle bushes shine their gold
In shade of a single tree.

✳ *Lillian M. Fisher*

REZ ROAD

The place we live isn't very big
compared to all that once was ours.
This reservation we call home
is ten miles long by six miles wide.
But even though it's not that large,
a nice new state superhighway
cuts through the middle of maple forest—
hunting grounds where we found medicine plants.

My Grampa Bigtree has always had
what our people call a really well
developed Indian sense of humor.
He says it all worked out for the best.
It's made hunting a whole lot easier
for us, although it now takes two—
one to stop traffic and one to run
out into the road to pick up game.
Although I know he's only kidding,
he's shown me how, if you know how to look,
you really can find our old healing plants
growing next to that four-lane road.

Sometimes tourists stray off the interstate
down onto Frog Street, where our Indian school,
box lacrosse field and meeting house
all crowd together with churches
and trailers and well-worn houses
in need of paint, some with cars
without wheels up on concrete blocks
parked like lawn ornaments in their front yards.

No one ever gets rich when they stay here.
Living on the rez, you learn how to share.
Tourists just don't see the things we see.
They're looking for tipis, chiefs in warbonnets,
not some dark-haired kid wearing sneakers
and headphones, bobbing his head to Indian Rap.

Yeah, things seem different
than they did long ago.
Some of our own people
don't even know how
to speak our language,
though we teach it in our school.
Some hit the road and don't come back.
But some of us, like Grampa Bigtree,
know that hidden roots still give you strength.

There will always be another day.
Four winds will always remember our names.
No matter how many roads they build,
Mother Earth is always beneath our feet.

✳ *Joseph Bruchac*

NEEDED

"Brandy, time to go," says Mom.
I hurry into coveralls, pull on my hat.
The back door whacks behind me.
It's a cold morning—stinging cold.

Dad loads our pickup with hay.
We can't afford a hired man this winter;
I'm only twelve, but *I* get to drive!
I slip behind the steering wheel.

When we reach north pasture, Dad jumps out,
climbs up on the load.
Tires crunch in crusty snow.
"Steer straight ahead," he calls.

Cows come running when they see our headlights
hooves stirring up clouds of crystals.
Steamy bodies crowd around us
shoving, bawling, stealing mouthfuls of hay.

"Speed up," shouts Dad. "Watch that ditch on your right!"
I press the gas, listen to the bale twine pop
as Dad splits open hay bales
pitching a trail of feed to hungry cows below.

When their bawling fades, I gear down
drive as slow as it goes.
The only sound is a low engine's growl.
"Stop," yells Dad. He hops inside the cab
bringing with him a sharp smell of hay.

＊ *Sandra Gilbert Brüg*

MOUNTAIN RAMBLE

I've roamed November hours on my winding mountain trail,
Dodged gust-flung tumbleweeds, observed an aimless rabbit track.
I've slogged through dust and underbrush, determined to prevail,
Rewarded by acquaintance with my tiring walk back.
In spite of unrelenting sun and punishing wind blowing,
I know, if briefly, where I am and where I plan on going.

✳ *Fran Haraway*

MILKING

The moon is up
but day is on the rise.

Half-asleep I set
my wobbly stool,
pat our big Holstein,
and begin to pull
milk down
from her warm-glove udder.

Soon I close my eyes
(keeping the milking rhythm)
and listen
to the barn—

One last cricket (hidden)
trilling away,
old boards creaking,
chickens speaking their foreign tongue,
grunting of a sleeping sow,
sweep of the cow's long tail,
warm milk stinging the inside
of my pail.

✳ *Tony Johnston*

LIVING ABOVE GOOD FORTUNE

I live above Good Fortune
where they catch crabs fresh

cook them any way you want
fast as you can spell c-r-u-s-t-a-c-e-a-n

I live around the corner from Heaven's Supermarket
where all lines are cash only

and you can get two for one
if you know to talk nice

I live on a street where every other thing is Lucky
and every other other thing is for tourists

My mother says,
"You don't want to go to those places"

even though she sees it in my eyes
how much I wish sometimes

but I live above Good Fortune
Lucky me

✻ *Janet S. Wong*

WALKING HOME FROM SCHOOL

Grandpa Stokes calls out from his porch,
"Your backpack looks mighty full."
"Just like always," I say.

Mrs. Sanchez, working in her garden, says,
"Take a flower to your mother."
I pick my favorite daffodil.

Mrs. Carter climbs into her van.
"I forgot something for supper."
I laugh and think, Again!

Julie Kim is on the telephone.
She gives me the thumbs-up sign.
That means her boyfriend's calling.

Mr. Potner hammers at his workbench.
"How's it going, Lauren?"
He asks the same thing every day.

On my street as far as I can see
I know everyone.
Everyone knows me.

❋ *Ann Whitford Paul*

CHRISTMAS TREE FARM

In April,
on our farm,
robins are first
to choose their trees.

All summer long
hummers zip, dip,
and hang suspended in the grove
like strings of lights.

On autumn nights
the last few fireflies
blink on and off
among evergreens.

Now, in cold December,
when summer things have flown,
I walk along the rows
with branches sweeping me
like brooms.

I peer inside a Douglas fir
where blisters on its trunk
are packages of sap
that smell like Christmas;

and I find twigs and thistledown
all woven in a ring:
a perfect Christmas ornament
robins made
last spring.

✳ *Alice Schertle*

CITY I LOVE

In the city
I live in—
city I love—
mornings wake
to
swishes, swashes,
sputters
of sweepers
swooshing litter
from gutters.

STREET

In the city
I live in—
city I love—
afternoons pulse
with
people hurrying,
scurrying—
races of faces
pacing to
must-get-there
places.

In the city
I live in—
city I love—
nights shimmer
with lights
competing
with stars
above
unknown heights.

In the city
I live in—
city I love—
as dreams
start to creep
my city
of senses
lulls
me
to
sleep.

✳ *Lee Bennett Hopkins*

ABOUT THE CONTRIBUTORS

JOSEPH BRUCHAC, an Abenaki Indian, is a renowned author, poet, and story-teller of Native American history and lore. He lives in Greenfield Center, New York.

SANDRA GILBERT BRÜG, a former teacher, is a children's librarian. Her poetry and short stories appear in many children's magazines and anthologies. She lives in Bozeman, Montana.

SHARON DARROW, recipient of The Society of Children's Book Writers and Illustrators Work-in-Progress Grant, is the author of several books for children. A college teacher, she lives in Chicago, Illinois.

REBECCA KAI DOTLICH, author of several books of poetry, lives and works in Carmel, Indiana. Since her debut as a poet in 1996, her work has appeared in numerous anthologies.

LILLIAN M. FISHER, author and poet, lives in Alpine, California, where she has the opportunity to explore the desert environment. She is interested in archaeology and has spent much time on reservations, studying Southwest Indian life.

JOAN BRANSFIELD GRAHAM grew up next to the Atlantic Ocean in New Jersey, and now lives near the Pacific Ocean in California. In addition to creating several books of concrete poetry, she is a frequent speaker in schools throughout the country.

FRAN HARAWAY, a native of Ohio, has lived in southern Nevada for over forty years. A retired high school teacher, she currently edits and writes biographies for the Nevada Women's History Project.

LEE BENNETT HOPKINS founded the Lee Bennett Hopkins Poetry Award administered by the Penn State College in Pennsylvania, given annually to a volume of poetry, and the Lee Bennett Hopkins/International Reading Association (IRA) Promising Poet Award, presented every three years by IRA. He spends a great deal of time in New York City, a place he truly loves.

PATRICIA HUBBELL has lived her entire life in Easton, Connecticut. Her career as a poet and author of numerous children's books spans close to four decades.

TONY JOHNSTON is the author of picture books and volumes of poetry. A former elementary school teacher, she is a quilter and a collector of antique Mexican furniture. She lives in San Marino, California.

C. DREW LAMM, a writing consultant, teacher, poet, and author of picture books and nonfiction works, lives with her daughter in Connecticut near salt water, where she dreams of spending nights on a houseboat.

ANN WHITFORD PAUL, author of picture books and poetry, is a teacher and avid quilter. Born in Evanston, Indiana, she now resides in Los Angeles, California.

ALICE SCHERTLE has created over thirty books for children after a career as an elementary school teacher. Born in California, she now lives on a Christmas tree farm in New England.

JANET S. WONG reflects on her Chinese/Korean heritage in much of her writing for children. A former lawyer, she lives in Medina, Washington.

JANE YOLEN is the highly acclaimed author of over two hundred books, including over twenty volumes of poetry. She divides her time between Hatfield, Massachusetts, and St. Andrews, Scotland.